M000209911

Thunderbird

Dorothea Lasky **𝕿𝖍𝖚𝖓𝖉𝖊𝖗𝖇𝖎𝖗𝖉**

Wave Books   Seattle and New York

PUBLISHED BY WAVE BOOKS

WWW.WAVEPOETRY.COM

COPYRIGHT © 2012 BY DOROTHEA LASKY

ALL RIGHTS RESERVED

WAVE BOOKS TITLES ARE DISTRIBUTED TO THE TRADE BY

CONSORTIUM BOOK SALES AND DISTRIBUTION

PHONE: 800/283/3572 | SAN 631/760X

THIS TITLE IS AVAILABLE IN LIMITED EDITION HARDCOVER

DIRECTLY FROM THE PUBLISHER

LIBRARY OF CONGRESS CATALOGING/IN/PUBLICATION DATA

LASKY, DOROTHEA, 1978–

THUNDERBIRD / DOROTHEA LASKY.—1ST ED.

P. CM.

POEMS.

ISBN 978/1/933517/63/6

I. TITLE.

PS3612.A858T48 2012

811′.6—DC23

2012001195

DESIGNED AND COMPOSED BY QUEMADURA

PRINTED IN THE UNITED STATES OF AMERICA

9 8 7 6 5 4 3 2 1

FIRST EDITION

WAVE BOOKS 032

I fancied you'd return the way you said,
But I grow old and I forget your name.
(I think I made you up inside my head.)

I should have loved a thunderbird instead;
At least when spring comes they roar back again.
I shut my eyes and all the world drops dead.
(I think I made you up inside my head.)

SYLVIA PLATH

Thunderbird

Baby of air

Baby of air
You rose into the mystical
Side of things
You could no longer live with us
We put you in a little home
Where they shut and locked the door
And at night
You blew out
And went wandering through the sea and sand
People cannot keep air in
I blow air in
I cannot keep it in
I read you a poem once
And you called it beauty
And then I read you another one and
You called it harmony air
My brother is not air, he is water
He is not a baby, he is older than me
And when he brushes the hair from my face
I cannot see him, but he surrounds me
I cannot see you baby of air
I put you in your bed and you get out

1

I put you in the air and you blend
I put you on the beach and you blow out
Like an air bird, flying and flying
I find other things similar to you
And like you, they are air and
Are nothing eventually
I am not made out of air
I hold your baby body in me
As I am a mother to you
I am a mother to you
My brother is my mother
He tells me when I have lost you
To grieve grieve
He says grieving is good
He says crying is good
He says sadness hits you in waves
Of water and air
I feel your fine hair hit me when I am sleeping
I feel your hair hit me in the head
Will you remember me
When you breeze upon the other world
O you are already there
O you are already there
My brother tells me, you are already there

He is already there, he says

And I cry

And he tells me

It is ok to cry

It is ok to cry,

He says

You are not made of air

It is ok to cry, he says

When you are not made of air

I had a man

Today when I was walking
I had a man tell me as he passed
That I was a white bitch (he was white)
And to not look at him
Or he was going to 'fuck me in my little butthole'
I wandered away
Who is to say
I think I am a white bitch
My butt is big
But I believe my butthole is little
This violence that we put on women
I don't think it's crazy
Someone I know said
'Oh, that man was crazy'
I don't think he was crazy
Maybe he could tell I had a look in my eye
That wasn't crazy anymore
Maybe he could feel the wild cool blood in me
And it frightened him
And he lashed out in fear
Maybe he knew I was the same as him
But had been born with this kind face and eyes

Doughlike appurtenances
What about the day I left
What happened then
Still I'm glad he said that to me
Still I'm glad he was so cruel to me
What bitter eye knew I had a voice
To say what men have done to me
What unkind wind has blown thru my brain
To make me speak for the wretched
To speak wretchedly about the ugly
To make my own face ugly and simple
To contort this simple smile into a haunting song

Is it murder

for Jasmine Fiore and Ryan Jenkins

What is murder
This is a very interesting poem to write
And to consider

I am coming from the devil
Living in the devil's house
Eating of the devil's food
Am I devil?

No
Large
Grey and red bird
Holy symmetrical
As in Asher
As in the book where it all started

What was evil?
I loved
And I loved truly
Yes
When I said I loved one

I loved another
When I said I was empty
I was indeed full

Take this bird
Large, green, itching my skin
To hold
Feathers that are liquid mice
At my touch
And eyes that are small round
Dragons
Take this room upon me
What is the purple motel
Where the bird lives?

That is the Thunderbird Motel
You go there on a plane
And land in a crash upon the pavement
And then you enter
And we die there again and again

When I am sitting on
This chair
I am staring at his dead body
From here

Writers make workshops
Artists make hell
To live in
I make hell to live in
I make hell

I make hell
Where it already is
In this poem

Long ago, when I loved a woman
Her name was Christine

She was blond
And in Canada

No

Long Ago I made this poem
And then you read it
And then I ate it

Word ectoplasm
Fiery meat that is liquid

Meat
Liquefied bites
Of meat that is your own

Was it the great murderer
Who made a man
Eat his own brain?

No
That man was not the best

I pour cinnamon into the
Ashes
Are you surprised when it all
Burns down

If I were not the
Devil would you
Not think I was evil
Either?

You are evil, Brother Red
The Snake is evil

All I want
In this life
Is for the Snake to
Leave me Alone

No

All I want in this Life
Is For the Words to leave me
Alone

I eat and eat them
And they become me

And you will never know
How much they are me

And when you peel my skin
Off me and
Take out my teeth
You will not see words

You will see fractals
That spell out letters

That spell out the words
Negative and Positive

Great Bird
Why do you leave me here on this earth?

I want to soar above clouds

Just today I saw a jet stream
And knew it was your yellow tail
I hear the rumble
Of your lightning tail
I see the symmetrical face
Of a great many lions
What half of their face is
Evil
And what half is
Good

Yes
It works
That way

No
It is The Doctrine of
The Similar

Which states that because
I am the same as you
I am both just as good and
Just as evil

Evil or
Good Bird
And
Red Brother
I am neither
Blue Sister
Nor the Absence
Of Fate

So what

So what

I was born into this life
And what a hell it was

To find me
Hanging
A dead
And living man
Meant to plow
Through all eternity

With no tool or
Force

Only my woman
Body
Meant to Die Again
And Again

Why it is a Black Life

Why is it a black life
Because nothing is permanent
And everything goes on and on not meaning anything
Because I am an animal
And I will always be displaced
Until I die
Because I am a human
And other humans will constantly think of new ways
     to kill me
And it will be loneliness until the end
Which will be more or less lonely
Because until then I eat by myself
And ignore everyone
Despite the fact that they look at me
With their empty eyeholes
And I read a book and am unable to nest with it
Because I say things
In the simplest way possible
And am constantly misunderstood
Because even when I mean well
I am still a criminal
And it is noon always

Hot sun beating on the blacktop
With the red bird endlessly flying
Because my feet and arms don't move
Unless I want them to
Because when they do
Move on their own
It is frightening
Because what is worse than terror
Is not terror
But health
Which is transitory
Which is often the worst friend of all
Because I sigh and sigh
And it sounds like a dog baying
And no one wants to help me
Because I am ugly, obnoxious, and insane
Because the only living things that like the sound of
    my voice
Are the vermin underneath the earth
Who are waiting for me to come join them

The world doesn't care

The world doesn't care if you pay your taxes on time
The world doesn't care

The world doesn't care if you are loved, hungry, or fed
The world doesn't care who died this year

The world doesn't care if you are murdered or raped
If you struggle, if you are generous

The world doesn't care if you are sad
If you are maimed

If no one believes in you
The world doesn't care

The world doesn't care if you grow up and the only thing
Keeping you in place
Is the devil

But I care
But I care if you are hungry

The world doesn't care
But I care

The world doesn't care
But I do

Death and Sylvia Plath

My student in the city college
Really likes the poems of Sylvia Plath
She is writing her research paper about
Lady Lazarus
I like this student
She spends some time
Leaning over me and telling me
How in the poem Plath turns from an object
Into an entertainer
And finally into a demon
Oh yes, you are right, I tell her
We are pleased
I wonder afterwards,
Why do young women like Sylvia Plath?
Why doesn't everyone?
The student tells me that when she was young
She liked Plath
I did too
I did not ride horses
Sylvia Plath rode horses
I don't have a thesis
I don't have a structure

I am a demon
There are blue streaks in the sky
It is Spring
I am not you
Nor do I want to be
It is 2:21 on 2/21/2010
I am not alive
No, I am no longer breathing
I don't live in this world
I already live in the other one

Misunderstood

I have come here today to say goodbye to my father
I feel somewhat understood and yet, misunderstood
I have drunk cool water under a large palm leaf
And now feel cool
I am not nervous anymore
Whatever death is
I am not nervous about it
It wasn't what we meant
When we first described pain
I just had a dream that
A woman's face was blown apart
By a plane crash
One side was normal
Her normal face
The other side was cut into, so that the muscle flapped
I saw the plane crash happen in my dream
Right after I had my usual dreams about betrayal
And as usual, the whole thing was off
It was not death I was after
Nor dreams
What is it in my words that makes
People think I care so much about dreams

What is it in my self that makes me think

I care so much about dreams

I don't care

About dreams

I care about this world

What is it about this world

That insists on making me feel so alone

So separate from it

When I drink a cool glass of water

Why do I feel so cool inside

In a way that is not representative of the outside world

What is it that when I am feverish

The rest of the world is not hot

What is it about this room

That makes me write a poem

And what is not a poem when I am out of it

People come and go

There are many ways men and women are taught to
   think about the world

I favor a world of fans

That push the air below you

At a breakneck pace

In my dream, I saw a face that was calm in not knowing
   it was blown apart

But instead of working against the odd feelings
I have of being so separate from you
I will be calm now in knowing we will never conjoin
I will think instead that yoking is all there is left to do
I will think instead of clouds and mountains
And put them in poems, not dreams
I will think of cool water that has some other sort of
    principle
In order to make me aware of my separateness
I will not think of love
Love is something that is too confusing
For understanding what is miscommunicated time
    and time again
In this world
I will not think of being born, which is too messy
A language
Or colors, that dot the landscape with emotions that I
    don't have the time nor space anymore to feel
Or beach or bed, I won't feel any of it
When I go to sleep I will wash linens and beans
    through the glow of an unearthly sun
Will it be a spirit that I will encounter then?
Yes. But it will be a new spirit, instead, that I will
    make myself

A rational spirit

A spirit who is always sure it knows and feels the land

A spirit who is not human, but has large arms

That I will walk along and on top of

And will not be sad anymore in their uncaring

Why go in cars

after Bernadette Mayer's
translation of Catullus #48

Why go in cars
They can be destroyed
I don't want to be destroyed by you
I love you and your want
We don't need cars
Why don't we sit in a sea of violets
I could kiss you a million times
And never be sick of it
Let's go sit in some flowers
Darling boy
Let's sit in a sea of flames
And I will never put the fire
Out of you

The Room

It rains incessantly
I go outside
I go inside
Inside the room are four ghosts
One is silent
One is old and another is young
Another preens himself upon the sofa
His hair is golden, there is a lyre
Women and men wait at his legs
Touching his airy cloak
He beckons me
I touch his face
What does it feel like? Nothing
I run from the room
Down the steps
Out the door
Down the street
I get on the nearest bus
I take that bus to a train
The train to a boat
I get on the boat
Then get on a larger one

I find a bedroom
It has a navy carpet
A red bed
I hide in yellow sheets
I fall asleep for days
When I wake
The golden man is next to me
Touching my face
Eyes going every which way
He tells me a story
It makes no sense
It is in a language that is like
My language, but is not mine
I remember I am American
I say, Is this America?
And he tells me that it is
In his hand appears a dish of ice cream
And when I eat the cold, dear liquid
I know I am already dead
I ask if I can at least go to heaven
Or to hell, whatever
Do I have to stay in this room with you forever, I ask him
He tells me I don't
That I can go anywhere

But that he and I are yoked
So wherever I go it will be with him
I punch him in the nose
I run down the hall of the boat
I jump into the water and flail
He saves me
He drags me to a beach
I come to
He ties me to his ankles
And sweeps me along to a house
That belonged to his family
He lays me in a maroon room
A male ghost appears
He is scraggly. I touch his face
I kiss him on the cheek
I run out the door
The golden man follows me
I run and run
My father appears as the feeling of a vision
And layers upon me
I am two ghosts
I stop and the man stops
And my father's ghost stops
And I look down and there is a hole

And I punch the man again
And my father and I go down into the hole
We slide down the hole for hours
My father is calm
Just stop, he says
I ask him if this is America
It is, the golden man says
As he catches us at the end of the hole
Where there is a room
With all my friends
By friends, I don't mean all of the people I've known
I mean all of the people I've truly loved
Smiling at me, everyone is calm
I sit down and they all come rushing at me
My father fastens me to a seat next to him
Am I still a witch, I ask them
My friend Conrad tells me we are still witches
One wall of the room drops
And turns into a giant face
The face is awful
I look into the eyes
I melt and scream
Then I am whole again
I am by a stream

There is a farm with animals
I have made this farm
I get up and tend to the fruit trees
And put the fruit in a basket
And in the background I hear children playing
And on the edge of my farm is a school
And the children are learning near my farm
And I go about it
And I go about it for a good long while

Everyone keeps me from my destiny

Everyone keeps me from my destiny
Keeps me from it
And keeps me locked away from beauty
And they can't feel my beauty
In me reaching out
Like glass into itself
And then into glass
And everyone keeps me from myself
Cause the self they had imagined
Was flesh and bone
And this flesh I am is glass
And everyone keeps me from my genius
Because genius is not human
And everyone wants me to be human
And I am not human
And everyone expects me to be something they are,
    which is human
And I can't be anything they are which is human
Because I am not human
And they are
And I am not human

This is a poem for you

How could this come to a good conclusion
I thought of your face, strange and French
And your sweater full of robins
You most likely think
I do not pay much attention
To your face
But I was sitting by the train
When inside I saw it burning
I'm sorry that some people
Think of this burning as nostalgia
Or sentimentality
And that we have to endure them
And that they are so boring
To want to think away everything
That is beautiful on this earth
I'm sorry that we have to think
Of other times when it might have been
More acceptable to burn
You were there
When I told you that a cold November
Would come
Wind and rain, the cold

May have hardened me
But there is not much else I am willing
To leave anything for but your
Face that is wet with wildflowers
The white wind, the warm wind
The cooling prisms above the beach
The beachtrees and scattered leaves
Above the Winter that will never come
I am not sure if we matter
I am not sure if your face matters
But I will destroy this house for it anyway
But I will scorch this black world for it anyway
Wet face and wild wind
I told you all it would come
This is a poem for you
This is a poem for all of you
Awful and quiet

I like weird ass hippies

I like weird ass hippies
And men with hairy backs
And small green animals
And organic milk
And chickens that hatch
Out of farms in Vermont
I like weird ass stuff
When we reach the other world
We will all be hippies
I like your weird ass spirit stick that you carry around
I like when you rub sage on my door
I like the lamb's blood you throw on my face
I like heaping sugar in a jar and saying a prayer
And then having it work
I like cursing out an enemy
And then cursing them in objects
Soaking their baby tooth in oil
Lighting it on fire with a tiny plastic horse
I like running through the fields of green
I am so caught up in flowers and fruit
I like shampooing my body
In strange potions you bought wholesale in Guatemala

I like when you rub your patchouli on me

And tell me I'm a man

I am a fucking man

A weird ass fucking man

If I didn't know any better I'd think I were Jesus or
    something

If I didn't know any better I'd sail to Ancient Greece

Wear sandals

Then go to Rome

Murder my daughter in front of the gods

Smoke powdered lapis

Carve pictographs into your dress

A thousand miles away from anything

When I die I will be a strange fucking hippie

And so will you

So will you

So get your cut-up heart away from

What you think you know

You know, we are all going away from here

At least have some human patience

For what lies on the other side

You are beautiful

You are beautiful
But you are also heartbreak
Locked forever frozen in time
A cry I cannot get out
No matter how much I grease myself
With honey
Pink palette of grapefruit, the book on the shoulder
Of the room, the rose gardens
But I do not want you to be so
I want to be spilling forth with the acid yellow honey
    of the bees
O love, take me thusforth
Into your secret places
I will never travel
I will never wake
You are more than heartbreak
In your fanciful suits and closing sighs
You are more than the shining blue room
On the afternoon of the date, the cold bite
You are the hot breath too I take myself into
The hot red fruit I take myself into
The living breathing thing I take in, I want to

Be a watery nymph in a wooded grove
With you
I want to be a cloud so full of honey
That there is nothing left of me
Until I throw myself into the fire
And am contained forever
I will be contained forever, a thing of beauty
Forever
I will be that thing forever
I don't want to be beautiful with you
I want to be an ugly, wretched, bleeding thing
Pouring out on the windmills
I want to be the locked tiger they can't lock up
Until it murders and then rages through the fields
Of wild grasses
I want to be so wild they can't lock me up
Put fences around me to pen me in
I will be so full of fire that they won't be able to
    extinguish me
Before the beauty comes I want to be so full of fire
That they can't tell me from you, my wretched angel
Sweet animal, they locked us in this life
But I think we still have time before we have to get
    out of it

Ugly Feelings

after Sianne Ngai

Why are people so cruel?
I mean that as a very serious question
Why can people be so cruel and why do they want to hurt
    other people
And why do they hate with such intensity
And why do normal things make normal people so mad

Matthew Savoca wrote in a poem
That Mother Nature is the new art
If that is true then what
Would that nature be
I really don't know

I really don't know
I'm serious—I don't
Oh, I am so stricken
Oh, I am so stricken with fear
When the evil comes around

Paranoia is the new art
A lump of deceit

Worry is the new art
And compulsion
And repulsion, an ugly heart

A voice is the new art
But it is rancid
A rancid tune
That I have worked out with care and concern
To make ragged

That you have worked out pitilessly
That you have striven for
That you have bent your fingers for
That you have come around to
Only to watch it come around again

Orange flowers in the grove
Are not ugly flowers
But they are dumb medals
Of the sun, who has watched them
Who has cured them in its heat

Only to watch them grow
Not birdless

But without birds
Not moonless
But to be a flower without a moon

Not a tree that has fallen with a lump of birds
But a moon that has fallen with a lump of birds
So that it is no longer a moon
So that its voice has no planetary pull
So, that there is no center

So, that center is beside the point
So that the tone is pain always
And hurt always
So that this life is always about
Dodging pain, but also inflicting it

And not a body
Not a body that feels
But a spirit that feels
A burned-out spirit
That is old and grey and small

And never renewed
Nor revived

That never has life
That is pageless and poreless
That is dead for all time

An ugliness has reached across this space
It is no feeling
But ugly feelings are the way we make of it
And what I say feelings are
Are feelings

And what I say are feelings
Are also not feelings
And what I say are old hurts
Are new hurts
And what deceit

And what deceit makes a moon go negative
And what black hole
Is the opposite of a rock
I only have you and me
I only have this hand to hold you with

And if I am an empty space
And if I am a truly empty space

Then my open hand is empty too
Then my heart a wide and open plain
Then my brain a dense infinity

A dense infinity of nothing
That holds no power
And if I hold no power
Then what ugliness could I truly hold
To make you so mad at me

To make you so cruel
And to extend that cruelty elsewhere
And if paper and bone make up light
And if animal fur makes up the night
And if light and earth are nothing

Then what is this light that shows my face?
Then, truly
I would rather it shroud in darkness
Then I would rather it always be dark
Then I would rather my open hand be night

For what love is useful
In this cold dark light

And what fire extends in this cold dark light
And what cruelty I will too create
In the cold dark night

And what cruelty will I extend
To your night
And what papery ghosts will I shove in your light
And what cold hand will I grasp your heart with
And what hot tag will I put upon your brain

You know a man told me a story once
Listen, listen
A man told me a story
It was
Of a toad

The toad was hungry
He was tired
He felt the swamp upon him
His felt his skin within him
He felt his black eyes melt with death

But he wasn't dead
And one day a child picked him up

And brought him with her
And made him a reptilian bed
In her house

Full of grasses and insects
Full of flowers, orange ones
And in the house was a painter
Who made a lovely picture
Of the toad and the girl

When the toad died
The girl died
Then I died
That's the story
I'm dead

Beautiful and ugly feelings
Gorgeous and horrific feelings
Feelings in the mouth of the cave
Feelings on the underbelly of the sun
Feelings that are hot and terrible

Listen, I am asking you
Why can people be so cruel

I really want to know
I want to know and I want you to know
And I want us to stop the reasons why

And I want us to reverse the earth
So that it is not possible
And I want us to pick each other up as animals
And for us to be friends
And I want us to sing and laugh

What falseness do you see
What falseness do you see
In a gentle exorcism
What ugliness do you see
In our quiet and watery laughter

That will cleanse the air
What ugly fountains might spring forth
From a watery and gentle laughter
That goes circling
Through the air

Zombies

Some people are zombies
Some people live with zombies
I live with a zombie
Zombies have flat affects
They are so frustrating
I turn into a demon
When I encounter
Blue-eyed nightmare
Curve my smile into its
What level water makes the eyeless eye
Oh yeah, that we are thrown out like trash
When we die
Oh yeah, that there is no elevation
And I throw myself in front of a train car
And again in front of the vehicle
Then in front of a plane
A boat, an endless thing
The sun burns out a corpse that is black and blue
And I live on with my own self
And I turn into a lyric when I see that zombie
And I turn ferocious when I meet that zombie because
The zombie is so much like me

But is the ugly parts of me, too
In that it has no style
No green operatic hat
And that it holds small brown lumps of dirt in its pockets
When in my own I hold the flowers
That I have picked from the zombie's pockets
To give to you

What poets should do

Poets should get back to saying crazy shit
All of the time
I am sick of academics or businesspeople telling poets
What we should do
A poet is a scientist
To favor poetry
Or science
In that both relate to Buddhism
However, both are things that melt
A purple haze or dawn
What sunken in
Always a shifting mood,
But it's true, I love you guys and gals
Of the wood and word
Let's say whatever it is we please
We don't have to defend anything
It is our God-given right to declaim
No, let me start again
It is our universal law to speak
Not an actuary to measure how thin
The arguments of our verse
To say we make a treatise in language, no

No we go on living and living and living on
That's beautiful, and poems are, too
Poems and shells
These little nothings I pick them up
All the livelong day
They are the signposts of comfort possible
To smooth the jagged edges
Of this worried traveler
That's what poems should do
And that's what poets actually do
Damn light
Always going on in my face
I just want a poem to speak of
So I go on and on
Into the night
And the townspeople, they say to you
That they may have seen
A monster
But no no I was only the dawn

Dog

for Lucy

When my dad was just a corpse
The man came and put him in a body bag
There was another man with dementia
Who had shared his room
The man recognized the black bag and got scared
I held him as they wheeled my dad away

Now I sit on the front steps with my dog
I tell her that nothing is permanent
So we should sit here and enjoy the cold air
That smells of other mammals
She sniffs and looks at me
I have my arm around her and start to cry

A neighbor comes up with her son
Who hides behind the building's corner
He is afraid of dogs
I take my dog into the building
We jump up the stairs
We are just two things in the air

I am the horse

I am the horse people should bet on
I am the person who will likely save you from a fire
I am the person who is black smoke
And blows black smoke in your eyes
I am the squeaky noise at night
I am the tables, and paper, and slugs
I am the thing that most excites you
I am the thing that most excites you
I am the horse that you should bet on
When you put your money down

Wild

Things are wild here
Everywhere around the green
Snakes, bobcats, and foxes
The purple flowers look wild
I am wild
My husband keeps me in his room so as not to upset
   the neighbors
The wildest thing about me is my arrogance
Which turns to anger
Over language
People put so much stock in wild language
I wander, an animal
Over hills
The civilized path, the orange sun
Do I dare mention God in this poem?
God is wild, and not human
And when people make God human
He stares at you through the eyes of a bear
And beats his terrible bearded chest
And guffaws into the stars
O the night, mysterious and purple
And the shining rocks

None of them are sins in their
Lack of humanity.
So why am I so horrible to look at,
With my wild hair
And my furry breast
And mouth

Plane crash of the Thunderbird

Bird, why did you come down the way that you do
Resting
Are you resting?
In the strange way
Of metal on skin
Burn
You were built to burn
And also
Sail through time and space
You flatten
Time and space
The big world
Why oh why bird, do we leave you
I want to be in you every day
I want to sleep in the belly of a silver metal bird
Every day
You can withstand the sky
The lightning crashes in you, you can withstand the
	lightning
The winds
The winds go in you, you can withstand the winds
You pull my hair

You put me up and down

You cause me to screech

I am a small bird in your belly

And willing I let you eat me, flying monster

And willing I submit to your heavens

Which are always circling in shadows, just beyond me

The Insurrection of
Satan as Thunderbird

I had this dream
That I was looking for this girl
To find her and feed her
And she was dead

I have known hatred
And hatred knows
No mercy

Satan is a flat orange snake
I hang him on my wall
And pray to him for forgiveness
But Satan knows no mercy
Satan, you know no mercy

What if I lost all those things

What if I lost all those things
Humor, wit, beauty
What if I lost it all
And there was nothing left of me
And what if I were just a corpse
And what if I were less than that
Would you still love me
Would you tunnel into the ground
Until the sun came out
So that you could have my body to hold
What if the sun were gone
Would you hold my body in the dead of night
Once he did
Once he did hold my body in the dead of night
If I forgot him then, will I forget him still
If I always loved him, will I love again
Dark night that is always calling
My body is thin paper to the air
We call conversation
Dark language
My body is dark red paper tonguing
The sun of the grave that I am in

Will you go tunneling through my grave
To find the setting sun
Will you go through my grave to get to another sun
One that is deep and blue
And fiery

To be the thing

To be the name uttered, but not to have the burden to be
To be the name said, but not heard
To not breathe anymore, to be the thing
To be the thing being breathed
To not be about to die, to be already dead
To not have to disappoint
To not have the burden of being late
Or punctual
To not eat, to not have to eat
To not feel anything
To not be the one whose affect is criticized
To not pick up the fallen⁄over boxes
To be everywhere but the boxes or plates
To not break the plates
To be beyond breaking
To have been broken
To not bear the burden of not being present
To not have to feel the pain of being hurt
To have transferred that pain over
So that hurt is only part of the imagination
And the imagination is everywhere, is every color
To not contain color, to be color

To not make sound, to be sound

To not have language, to echo, to plan language

To be the stream of words

To not be sad for

To not have those be sad for

To not eat alone

To not fuck those who do not find your corpse attractive

To not fuck

Or stuff

To be ashes and non-placed

Not displaced, but to not be in any place

To enter the ocean on not a whim, but a physical force

Where there is no center

Where there is no safety

There never was

There was never any anger

There was never anything to look at

I never looked at anything

I just went and walked

I tried to love

But love is hopeless

And I have lost all hope, so bleak I am beyond

I am beyond what might be considered low

There is no low nor high, space or time, I have

Gone away from that which is uttered
I have not burdened to be spoken of or spoken for
To croak every day to the livelong bog
I do not speak a thing
I exist
No, no I don't
I never did
And you may have
But I never did
And you may have called out for me
But I was already gone
And I am already there
That which you speak of
I am already spoken for
In a world of light and ashes
They all call my name
They have waited for me
And now I know
I was always
Already there
With them

Take care of yourself Alice

Everything is trauma
Everything takes away from the center
Even the cops Alice
Who I think are there to protect me
Even though cops are never there to protect you
Even though men are selfish and brutish
Even though
The men are like they are
I keep looking into those cops' faces like one would
   save me
Even though they will never save me
Even though

I will come and meet you Alice
By the woods or dock
Poor Alice
You have a psychopath harassing you
And now me

Now me
I am no lion
I have no relationship to you

Except for me to tell you you are rare
Or that your reaction is rare
Or that it is
When you told him
To leave you alone

I myself
Have spent a whole lifetime
Never telling anyone to leave me alone

But always
Wanting to
Always wanting to get back to the center
Where I was born

Dear Alice
Poor Alice
Was it a dream when we first met
Whatever it was
I'll wait for you by the rain

Be wearing that
Dress, be combing that

Hair
Be knocking that door

The door of rock and slate
The door of forgiveness
And superstition

Be holding that bouquet
Of death tokens
Be looking this way
And that

I want to be dead

I want to be dead
After all the ultimate act of self-indulgence is to be dead
Histrionic bareback

Middle-aged men are the devils I shall meet
When I'm dead
In this life I was a middle-aged middle-class middle-of-
   the-road woman
Middlemen are the exorcised demons of my death

What could be more dramatic than a last breath?
This breath
No that one
No what do I make of it

All of you
All of you are so boring
You are living
Eating, breathing, pissing
Waiting to know when it all will happen

I am already dead
I want to be dead
I am already dead
I am already fucking words

I am already words
That paint this page
Peppery black specks

Move me around
Tear up this paper
Burn this paper

Light this paper on fire

I don't care

I am already dead

Whatever form you make of me
I will always come back to this one

Gender

It took me a long time to realize that my anger was a
    gendered one
Flat soda on a Saturday morning
The men and women did it better than I ever will
I tend to think that I should just stop
Purple lamppost
And pushing my head into it
Anthony, my friend, writes poems about vaginas
And what space they entail—this life
I write poems about boobs and dicks
But my anger comes not from this
But from being silenced
So that I hate what they like
Not listening to me
So that I could go on and on
And it sounds like nothing
Which is the worst thing of all
No, not to not have a voice anymore
But to have a voice in its entirety
Never going away
Or this way or that way
Again

Who to tell

Who to tell no one cares when no one cares
No one takes the time to care for a monster

I care for monsters
But only because I am one

I go in the dark house
With the ghosts
And the ghosts take my coat off
The junkies

The other man sits slumped in the chair
Is he dead yet?
I do not know

I know that no one cares about anything
I do know that the dressing room
Is drab and grey

And my pink patterned dress
Looks ridiculous against something so truthful

Wildness is not sadness
The wilderness is not sad
It is naked

I am not
If only because
Decomposition is
Not nudity

Who to tell this?
Who do I tell when no one cares

I did not expect them to
I did not expect them to care
I am not mad

I'm not mad any longer
People eat tomatoes
People eat bread

I am a monster
I eat life

But only because I am losing mine
Into a horrible void
That for you is only an idea

I once felt better about things
I once felt better about things
When the blankness was just an idea
Like the way you still think of it

Still I don't think love is an idea
I don't think compassion is an idea
I don't think babies are born out of loneliness
I don't think the sea is cold

I only think it is cool
Cool cool sea
Blue-green mystery
Mysterious fish

If only I had been born
A fish
Instead of a monster

If only the water were my only home
I would swim so quietly
I would not say hello to you
I would no longer be sad

I would still be me though
And I would not let you catch me
For your dinner

And when you wanted to eat me for your dinner
I would disappear

Two assholes

I got caught in the scheme of two assholes
But I was too far in their scheme to see my way out of it
So all I did was wait
Until the woman's suggestions seemed sort of sensible
I was so caught up in the poem
That the nice guy behind me on the street startled me
    with his walking
Until I became the antichrist
I write better when I am on my period
But I don't mean that I am a feminist
I mean that when I am a certain way
Certain words come out
And I am susceptible to the great rhythms
And the great rhythms of seeing
Like when I read the woman's words
I found them undeniably a cultivated kind of quirky
That comes from an educated style of smartness
Likely a sort of snobbishness
But also, a real understanding of what sells
I do not sell
But that is a good thing
I go month after month the earthly thing I became

When I entered this world
While other people become more and more
Plastic and unspiritual
I am not what this world needs
I will never interact with the world
In the way it needs me to
But I will never apologize for this at all
The red light hangs in the neighbor's window
On the street there are the men that have inhabited my
    nightmares
All dressed up in earthly clothes
Somewhere five miles away are people I will get
All wrapped up in their lives and then they will forget
    about me
In six years I will have two children whose names will
    escape me
As I will escape into the great disease that took my father
The great disease where your mind is the worst thing to go

Love Song to the night

I am remembering my old self, but that old self is dead
And all those people who knew me then
Well they should mourn and mourn
Because the self I am now
Is more an encroaching sense of nothingness than they
    might realize

Dear sweet Clodia
I met you by the dock
You had on a blue dress and you knew me
You will not know me anymore
When you see me

My face is not the same
And moreover, it is old
Except when we see each other in the afterworld
I think then you will know me
And will turn your head this way

And that way
Your curls and heart purpled
You giving tension to the cord

How damaging
That this will be the only way

You will know to love me again
After all of this, after all of this is over

The Enemy

The Enemy makes an enemy
Of another person
Because the Enemy is within her
I screamed I hollered
I cannot make the Snake get
From within me
He screamed he hollered
He wanted the Enemy out
She screamed she hollered
She wanted the Enemy out of the house
She wanted to destroy what the Enemy had
The other person is not the Enemy
When you want to destroy the Enemy
You must realize that you are the Enemy
I want everyone to like me
It is because I am the Enemy
The Enemy only wants to self-destruct
In order to kill the Enemy
I only want to make a prison out of this home
To keep the Enemy out
But it is really to keep the Enemy within borders
Except that the borders are within the borders

There is no air that flows through my lungs
That has not been processed by the Enemy's air
There is no pure air that has not been
Made into another air
Which would be that of the Enemy's
Where did he go?
Did he go to the Enemy?
Did he dissolve into the Enemy?
I wrote poem after poem about him
I had a dream, and then another
Was the dream what the Enemy put in?
Was the Enemy trying to make my air
Roll over into his place, by tempting me with the dream?
Did the Snake dance around in place
And make the Enemy so that I would never know
The Enemy is within me, but within him
Do I want to murder the Enemy
So that I don't want to murder myself
When I murder the Enemy
I do also murder myself
Did the Enemy make pain
So that I would distinguish my own Enemy from yours
Whatever, I want to leap and walk
I want to walk boundless

Whatever whatever, I want solar chaos
I am sick, I want health
I want the flowers to be made sinister
With air from the Enemy
The flowers, in their red bell heads
Were always the Enemy
Put the Enemy on your table now
Children, lovers, friends
Decorate your room with the Enemy's tulips
The Enemy will brighten the room

Cortex

Cerebral cortex
The plane of personality

Winged green mating
Wrapped in green sheets
Rolled in green hair
The yellow ringing

The best revenge

The best revenge is
To make someone
Turn upon themselves

The best revenge
Is to make the group
Outside of you think
The person in question
Has done something wrong

Revenge is housed in the cortex
Just like the personality

Deep dark red
Animal

Green Anthony
And Red Anthony

You are my muse
Ridiculous and wild
Voice from the earth

The bourgeoisie covet the wild
The bourgeoisie covet the wild
And the bobcat
I can still remember my dream
And the man, the bees

I can still remember my wild dream
My cerebellum made
And made me move through

The best thing you can do is to leave me alone
The best thing the Snake can do is to leave me alone

I was quiet
I wanted to be left alone
I was quiet I wanted to be left alone
I can be ferocious when I am not left alone

Leave her alone he told me she is an old woman
He told me, to leave her alone, she is an old woman

Of course I would, she is Rangda
Of course I would I told him
The woman is Rangda

She is my enemy, the worst demon of all
Turning in on herself
Turn in on yourself, faithful widow
Electric snake, and wild blue hair

Windows of light opening
Into light that is faint yellow
And then dark red

And then full and material
Material light
That is ectoplasm

Wretched face in the morning light
O wretched face
Teeth of the animal, and eyes of the self

The best revenge
Is to draw two things similar
So that they are the same

Core green and red
Similar brain core
What makes personality
And the social

Rangda is not the cortex of the brain
But without her there is no revenge
There is no enemy
Without her there is no light

No heavens
No blue no red
No green no yellow
No sound

Without Rangda
There is no sound
Heavy bells

Heavy bellows from sky
Without Rangda
There are no bells nor sky
Without Rangda, there is no sky

How I Started off

When I was a young poet
I started off loving the thing more than the people
It took me a long time
But then I loved the thing so much that I loved the people
    that made it
What now?
I love the people
More than the thing
I don't love words
People love the things
More
They love the words more
Like you
You love the words more
Hey hey Rangda
Hey Rangda hey

Reality

You speak of one reality
I speak of another

Not alternate or surreal
But one that is parallel or recurring

Endlessly making one piece of me
Into another thing

You think of this world
I am in the next

I know the white world
Where I have no eyes

I know what it is like
To float without space

A jellied formless being
That ceases to know time and context

That is not condescending to the material
But knows it is a one-sided line

And that the infinite is a radiating set of lines
And that we only walk around seamlessly

On this one

Death of the Polish empire

I.

I got sad when it happened
The plane crash
Down in a field of trees
The trees the things that touched the wings
The melting head, the fireball
The thing landing as just a thing

Poland is dead and I am not already

I'd like to take this opportunity before I begin
To thank the editors
For including me in their anthology
But I must also tell them
That I do not want to be feminine anymore

I am judiciously silent
Until I have something important
Really important to say

About females—no I don't
Drip, drop, about it I do not

But not because it is not important
Not because females are not important
But because I really have nothing to say

I am overwhelmed
I am not grotesque, nor kitsch, nor cutesy
I just went to the 7-Eleven and felt more
Comfortable there than in the Whole Foods
What does that say about me?

It is not my birthday today, but I will die
But maybe not in a plane crash
But maybe not ever
But maybe I will never die
Oh you think not
Oh you do not think so
Oh what do you know

Piercing gaze
You read this poem
I don't care if you are male or female
What your age might be
Where you are from
I don't care

I think it is all silly
Your gaze is hot on my neck
Telling me to write things
Telling me that if I write things a certain way
You may or may not
Read them

What or whom am I writing for?
The Polish empire is dead today
My father died six weeks ago
I have no real anything to speak of
I am not a body anymore when you read this
What am I then
I am what I was made visible.
What am I then
I am the word

II.

They say it happened because the pilots did not stop
When they were supposed to
The pilots were supposed to stop
Because of the fog
And that they instructed them to do so
They say they instructed them to do so

But that they could not insist
They say they could not insist
Oh what do they know

Dumb pilots, they tried to land
They were too low
The fog blinded their sight
Political figures
Brutish pilots
JFK Jr. in the open sea
At night in fog
To go sailing
He got too low and flipped
Dumb pilots, you are dead
You got too low
Your wings touched the trees
You lost lift immediately, you crashed
Almost 100 people died
You died, too

100 people,
But who were they
The entire Roman,
I mean Polish,

Empire
The entire Polish empire
The entire regime died today
I did not die

It is all so far off, I know
I know
I know it is 2015 when you are reading this
It is all so far off
I know we are dead when we are reading this again
I know it is all so far off
I know

The 20,000 people who were massacred
Who they were flying the plane in
To go, get out of, and commemorate the dead
I know that those people
Are far off, too
Yes, I know

When we are feeling fine
When we wake up, read a poem like this one,
Go back to sleep, or rise,
Eat something, look out the window

I know when we all seem fine
That it is easy not to understand

But you are one thing
If you died
The whole world would be less
When 100 people die
The world is less
It is not ok
When 20,000 people are murdered
It is not ok
When the woman in Florida accidentally
Murders her baby it is not ok
I am in this room
I am in my coffin
My father, a holy man
In a coffin
It is not ok

When you think it is
When you think other things are important
When you make sex the important thing
And not death
Then I have no time for you

When you live a life and write
And believe that sex and gender are the defining things
Then I have no time for you
I will have nothing to say

Death is what defines a poem
The poem is dead
Always dead
You want to know what makes a poem special?
It is dead
Writing is there
It is dead
Horses are magical
Planes fly
The flowers are beautiful
Writing is death
The poem is dead
It was always dead
Respect poems
Respect this poem
It is dead
And you are dead
And I am dead
And when we talk and kiss and eat
We do it on a dead timeline

Which is the history of the world
Which is something like fate
Which if we were only able to really understand
We would know
Is something more like physics

III.

I am tired now
They say the flower died there before
On the cursed land
Let's look at the flower again
Before we fade away

The white flower
Was born out of dew
Parents who were water and air
Two or three green bulbs
The sun
The air

Would you like to think of its petals?
They were white, with yellow flakes
And also green
In the fog you could see the yellow flakes
Just before they burst into flames

What else matters but the stage

Nothing matters but the stage
I don't do anything if not to show it off
What is that eye if not for to be looked upon
I breathe and it is to be applauded for
I learn these things, so that I can retell them
What is memory
If not to remember so that
Another can recall
O life goes endlessly endlessly down a blue ravine
But I am back
And I got your attention
So what else matters
I moved this arm
And leg
Just so that you might look at me

Genius

If I believed in genius, then I'd say
Yes I am one
But I don't believe, believe in it
Nor intelligence
Or all that
Why? Because it is fostered
Determined
It is not born
It is not a magical spell
There is no muse
There are only the wild wild forces
That are allowed in
The strange angels
The cold head
The cold head of the poem
Blown right off
Into another's head
And the things that made that happen
Like wealth? Yeah sure
Like wealth
Of course, like wealth
And time and money (not just wealth)

And rich art to immerse one's self in
And life
Horrible life, and the sweet things, too
And freedom
And being told it is ok to feel
And to feel like you are a great person
Because, Goddamn you, everyone is
A person and everyone can be a great person
Of course, they can
If they want to be
But knowing a thing
Knowledge
And language
Knowledge and language
Are nothing
They are sounds
Made from the animal
To alert, to tend to
To make happen
Big ideas
Are things to build
To construct
We are one thing
It is easy to understand

This is easy to understand
Genius is easy to understand
It means to build
Evil is the opposite
Although genius and evil can come together
Evil is the torn down
Not feeling great
Feeling like death is the plight of the individual
It's not
Genius is for everyone
The stars are for everyone
Dark blood is an infinite regress
To black infinity
Which is so dark it is one light
To feel means not to see
To see is not to feel
To know is nothing
And genius is not knowing
It is feeling
It is feeling out
It is feeling out you out there
It is feeling out oblivion

Time

A woman in all red walks past me with her two white
    dogs in red sweaters
I walk past in all blue with a black dog
I cannot get away from the idea that time is not linear
And that emotion makes us reach a moment where it
    happens all at once
But not a moment
My love says this knowledge of mine is the most basic:
    a given
Something we are left with
He will never lose anyone the way I have
He will never lose me until I am dead
You and I, my reader, we exist in a timeless way
Always in space and time together
I do not touch you
But I write these words to you
Out of love, or hate, or both
What grand a feeling I feel for you
And yet it is very small
In the utter blackness
Or blankness
Where an all-emotional head

Lifts two green eyes with a dark heart
I am not sure if it is this head, or you,
Who speaks to me
I know I am lost forever, floating
Forever fragmented
And that this either brings me comfort or despair, or both
Because I know that you and I will never be together
Such a vast and endless sense of nothingness
For this alone, I speak

Odd feelings

I have odd feelings
I do not know where they come from

I used to write things down
I used to fish for words

Now I fish for the almighty figure of the wood
The woodcock, or black root

The red sky
It all gives me a strange feeling

I used to seek this out
Now I drive my blue car

Down one road just to go to the other
The silver snake picks me up and

My body is my anger vehicle
A murderer into the air

I go, not wild but the opposite
Of silence

Or to not be better not to interact
But to be a floating thing

Purple land orb
Green tissue in the wind

That was once my own eye
Many lifetimes ago

But is now my only eye
That travels from hill to hill

In spite of everything

The Rose

I smelled the rose first
Whatever it was, I didn't care anymore
I went home
But there was nothing like that
There is the taking your hair down
In a group of roses
And the little flags the angels adorn
But what legs
And back did you scream into
There was no house
There was no home
There were only relations of time
That put this body
Into your very easily vacuous and facile one
The petal upon
Folding over
Until I couldn't see anymore
I love poetry
And in every way
This smites me
So I don't
Really think

I'll come home again
I think I'll go out walking
And lose
I will lose myself again
And in what else:
Birth and breath
And birth and Spring

The changing of the seasons
is life and death seen gently

Hello, The changing of the seasons is life and death
   seen gently,
Hello
Hello there
It ebbs and flows
I saw Fall go quietly into Winter
It is not like death
Green to yellow to orange to red to black
To a final white
It is not skin to blue
Fullness to stiffness
It is not the same
As a breeze that is one day colder
Maybe just slightly colder
Until the final cold
The eye of death goes out
It is life going out
The seasons happen gently, hello
Life does not
Brash, unexpected
It happens dramatically

Hatred, love
Murder, sex
It happens in a sort of violence
The seasons are not violent
The changing of the seasons is not a storm
You there
You will not go gently
And why should you?
The seasons they happen gently
They happen gently
Softly
And why shouldn't they?
Why shouldn't they, I ask you?
They know they will come again

Thank you to the editors of the following journals for first publishing some of the poems in this book: *American Poet*, *The Awl*, *The Baffler*, *Coldfront Magazine*, *Columbia Poetry Review*, *Dewclaw*, *Diode Poetry Journal*, *Gulf Coast*, *Maggy*, *MARY: A Journal of New Writing*, *Mrs. Maybe*, *The Paris Review*, *Peacock Online Review*, *Poetry Northwest*, *Poor Claudia*, *Sink Review*, *Sixth Finch*, *Supermachine Journal*, and *Tin House*. Thank you to Iris Cushing and everyone at Argos Books, who originally published portions of this book in a chapbook titled *Matter: A Picturebook*, alongside paintings by Matthew Fischer. Thank you to Katherine Sullivan and everyone at YesYes Books for publishing a chapbook of sister poems to this book, called *The Blue Teratorn*. Thank you to Francesca Chabrier and everyone at Flying Object for selecting my poem, "Misunderstood," and turning it into a broadside for their It's My Decision series. Thank you to CAConrad for featuring "The Room" on his *Jupiter 88* video series. Thank you to Zachary Pace and everyone at *THEthe Poetry* for featuring my poem "Who to tell" in their Poem of the Week series. Thank you to Joshua Beckman for his invaluable counsel on this book and to everyone at Wave Books, for making this book possible. Special thanks to my family and friends for their inspiration, care, and support.